AN ARBORIST POINT OF VIEW FROM UNDER THE CANOPY

Marc A. Goldberg born in Boston, Massachusetts grew up in the suburbs finding solace in anything outdoors. A boy who couldn't sit still found his inner peace in nature hiking the most overgrown trails and climbing into many a tree. Marc seemed to always have his share of scratches, mosquito bites and poison ivy from a day in the woods.

As a young adult Marc wrote many thoughts about his life on napkins, scrap paper, note pads, cardboard or receipts and continued to pen his views as an Arborist.

In this book (Marcs' first book) An Arborist Point of View from Under the Canopy Marc shares his dreams, ideas, thoughts and perceptions in hopes that it inspires everyone to chase their dreams. This book is a testament of an adult who wrestled with stepping outside his comfort zone and finally sharing his thoughts that he placed in a box for over 35 years.

COPYRIGHTS

Registration Number: TXu 2-440-355

Effective Date of Registration

July 20, 24

Registration Decision Date:

August 05, 2024

Copyright Registration for One Work by One Author

Registration issued pursuant to 37 CFR $202.3

An Arborist Point of View from under the canopy.

Year of Completion: 2023

Author: Marc Andrew Goldberg

Author Created: Nonfiction Work

Citizen of: United States

Copy Claimants: Marc Andrew Goldberg

Date: July 20, 2024

DEDICATION:

Robert "Bob" Morissette:

You inspired me to chase my dreams and believed in me when I didn't believe in myself.

ACKNOWLEDGEMENTS

I would like to thank my wife Valerie and my gaggle of kids Indy, Ethan, Chesca, Brodie and Ellery whose honesty humbles me and are my biggest fans! A shout out to my furry friend Shay the Border Collie who has never been tired out but "dogpressed" when the balls aren't being thrown.

Being amongst trees for over 20 years as an ISA Certified Arborist I had lots of time to ponder as I walked under the canopies of San Diegos Urban Forests. My ideas and thoughts even surprised me, which I credit the trees who have always talked to me. I hope some of my ideas bring a different perspective, aid you in troubling times and push you forward to achieving your goals.

FOREWORD
Urban Forest – my
observations and opinions

In metropolitan environments arborists refer to the trees within a certain area (Apartment Complexes, Homeowner Associations and Parks) as an Urban Forest. Even though an urban forest doesn't act biologically as a true natural forest it does help with carbon sequestering, reduction of air pollution, air and asphalt cooling, reduction of crimes, cooling of buildings and reducing urban water runoff. Urban Forest trees tend to act independently and are more in need of humans to assist in their health than a true natural forest.

A natural forest and an urban forest both sequester carbon and clean our air but were created differently. One was created by Gods' hand while the other was created by man for aesthetic purposes. One was created to be self-reliant while the other is at the mercy and hand of humans. One has trees that work together and communicate with each other through their purposely entangled root systems while the other is full of individual species that don't seem to interact with such complexity.

An urban forest are individual trees brought together for the benefit of landscape aesthetics, camouflaging of buildings and shade yet not usually in the best interest of the tree but the best interest of man. Don't get me wrong my career as an Arborist was built on maintaining individual trees but my heart wonders and at times believes I manage an orphanage of trees that truly are sad and used for someone else's goals which are not in the best interest of the tree.

Sometimes urban forests look like natural forests. An example would be a large city park where there are no buildings and vehicles are not accessible. These urban forests begin to act as true natural forests where individual trees begin to work together and flourish.

Urban forests have the strongest individual trees. Every day tortured by the lack of growing space for their canopy and/or space for their roots within the ground they are force-fed pollution from water runoff. Their own leaves covered in the silt of air pollution affect the transpiration of water through their stomata and the ability to create photosynthesis. The urban forest trees' own roots are girdled (side affects from being left in their nursery container too long) and when those girdled roots are not pruned off before the tree is planted it creates an unsteady, unhealthy, and diseased prone tree that will struggle to maturity. The urban forest trees are planted within our human-created landscapes which may not be in the best interest of the tree due to incorrect soil type and growing space. The urban forest trees are sometimes vandalized with sharp objects so humans can see their initials on the tree's bark and/or painted with graffiti to make a statement. Most urban trees are severely overwatered or underwatered and are truly not managed correctly. Sometimes tree stakes installed during installation to help the tree stand on its own are not managed and become entangled with the supportive tree ties chocking the tree around its trunk causing more damage than nurture.

Born in Boston, Massachusetts my family moved to the suburbs when I was young. My father who can sell a wool jacket to a sheep and a love for furniture (2nd generation furniture salesman) brought his talents to the wooded suburbs. I grew up playing in the forest yet at the same time construction and urbanization were changing our quiet town into a popular suburb destination. As I grew up tree canopies disappeared while concert venues, golf courses, new homes, shopping centers, industrial parks and much more ate away at my outdoor playgrounds.

The happiest places for me growing up as a young child and the best memories I ever had were walking amongst a tree or trees. When I was seven my first kiss was in my backyard aloft in a sycamore tree. I didn't know it then but the kiss confirmed I was happiest amongst one of God's greatest creations. As I grew older, I was pulled towards trees indirectly and directly every day of my life. Every life decision I have made as I look back through my life included trees:

-Started landscaping in my teens

-Attended Unity Environmental University (Unity College)

-Became an ISA Certified Arborist in my early 30s

-Named two of my children after trees

-Traveled with my children on our first vacation as a single father to Sequoia National Park

-Every vacation included a tree element or tree visit and still due to this day

-At our wedding my wife Val and I created table decor utilizing miscellaneous tree pieces that included pinecones and branches.

-My Honeymoon found me in Hawaii on the Big Island under giant Ficus trees

-My midlife crisis was put to rest while touching fungi, walking through meadows and being massaged by rustling leaves of birch trees in the forests of New Hampshire.

 All landscapes that I built or designed were around the trees first. For me the greatest landscapes are built around trees and the focal point of all landscapes are the trees. I always had an inner pull towards a tree, to be amongst the trees to look at trees.

As you read through my book I hope you enjoy my photos, observations and opinions of my life amongst trees.

*1   Your dreams and goals are only
controlled by your effort not the
opinions of others- continue to be
you.*

*2   The crown of righteousness lies
heavily on your head, but walking
with no purpose is a heavier burden
on your conscience.*

*3   Sometimes it takes stupid people to
wake up smart people doing stupid
things.*

4   What each parent needs to understand:

Parenting-

Not for the faint of heart

Nor the weak

Nor those with thin skin

Or no patience

OK with saying NO

And not being popular

Or cool

Or liked

You will be ignored

Lied to

Talked back at

Criticized

And of course misunderstood

But

Knowing we can help shape

Mold

And Guide

Makes this journey - a journey worth

taking

5   Don't define your happiness by someone else's thoughts.

6   Drugs are a temporary pill that numbs regrets.

7   Success isn't knowing all the answers, it's surrounding yourself with people who can help you find those answers.

8   Human growth is appreciating each failure because it takes you closer to your successes.

9   Even though the sky is gray it's
always sunny because I have you.
You're my light when it's dark. You're
my compass when I'm lost. You're
my life jacket when I'm overboard.
You're my roof in a rainstorm. You're
my partner when all have given up.
You're my best friend. You're my
better half.

10 A clock never turns back. Father
time won't stop the clock. Time is
a commodity that you can trade or
sell but at what cost when the
clock runs out.

11 ***The only limitation in life is the limitations we put on ourselves***.

12 ***Education is great, intelligence is better but being persistent is the magical dust that makes dreams reality.***

13 ***All successful athletes have (CSM) Conditioning, Skillset, Mindset***

14 I wake up every day a better man because I laid down with you yesterday.

15 Trees appreciate their roots.

16 I am a fan of more trees and less assholes.

17 You will be defined by the way you treat people not the amount of money in your pocket.

18 Remember Me.

Not for my material but memories we made.

Not for what I acquired but for my actions.

Not for my uneasiness but for my uniqueness.

Not for my imperfections but our perfect moments.

Not for what we didn't finish but our finishes!

19 What defines us and what we are remembered by will be our actions and thoughts not what we owned.

20 Be remembered for how we helped not what we had.

21 Memories we made will always walk along my side even when you're gone.

22 Enjoy the ride because life is a one-way trip.

*23 A gravel road is bumpy and uneven
but never corrupt or forged.*

*24 Live life with intentionality- with a
compass and game plan in
handopportunities will become
endless.*

25 Think of others when making decisions.

26 People are like trees, sometimes they stump us.

27 You can't force someone to dance.

28 The biggest competition we have is ourselves.

*29 Everyone should watch the sunset
and sunrise every day because it
will remind us there is something
bigger and more important than us.*

*30 A walk in an Urban Forest shows
the true grit of a tree.*

*31 Losing a friend may be the painful
catalyst that fuels you to chase
down your broken dreams.*

*32 Your value isn't what others think
but rather how you think about
yourself.*

*33 I'd rather walk on honest jagged
rocks than travel over lies laying on
pillows.*

*34 Democracy was created where all
laws are applied equally;
unfortunately, when not enforced
breeds anarchy.*

*35 I refuse to look back at what happened
and eagerly look forward to what is
possible.*

36 Health is the true measure of our wealth yet overlooked in the pursuit of the dollar.

37 Stop leaning on your weaknesses and lean on your strengths.

38 The only person that can control how you feel is you.

39 Set your compass to where you want to go not where others want you to walk.

40 *Your life is your journey so without apologies blaze your own trail.*

41 When we require other people's validation to feel happy it's like we are chasing that mythical pot of gold at the end of the rainbow.

42 No one is allowed to judge you or break you.

43 *Funny how Mother Nature slowly takes back what we don't want anymore.*

44 *Every step I walk is easier with my loved ones by my side.*

45 My small patio garden creates an oasis for many creatures, my favorite Gnomes and more important a place to recharge my battery.

*46 Remember your family and friends
are always walking with you on
your journey.*

*47 On Labor Day I appreciate the time
to enjoy the trees along my favorite
hiking trail.*

48 Define yourself without the pictures others have drawn.

49 I remember I used to make fun of AARP (American Association of Retired Persons) and now I am excited to join.

50 What one says and what one does says everything about the individual.

51 *The power of being bilingual is an awesome tool to have in your toolbelt.*

52 *There is a lot of traffic on the road ahead but our destination isn't as important as the guidance we will provide to our passengers in the back seat.*

53 *If there is a silver lining to all the chaos in this world it is knowing I have you*.

54 When I look at you I'm reminded how lucky I am to have you as my wife on this trip we call life.

55 If I didn't say I loved you today then I am the fool.

56 Health is the most unappreciated yet is the totality of what we are.

*57 Problems are what we create when
we don't want to deal with reality.*

*58 A walk through the woods puts life
into perspective.*

59 A true-life cycle is a forest.

*60 Smart people are not always
successful – successful people are
not always smart.*

*61 Many smart people never reach their
potential because they are afraid of
failing.*

*62 Live life as though you are not
guaranteed tomorrow and only then
will you look deep inside your soul and
reach for the stars not wait for them to
fall onto you.*

63 *Seconds turn into minutes, minutes turn into hours, hours turn into days, days into weeks, weeks into months, months into years and years feel like seconds.*

64 *Advice from my grandfather Charles Stone "Listen, Look, Smell and when you want to say something- DON'T".*

65 *Listening is when you hear and have no advice.*

66 *I'm not sure why this door is closing or won't let you in but I do believe a door will open for you when life is ready to let you in. Whatever decision you make remember those who don't believe in you are not allowed to steal your confidence nor your inner strength.*

67 *As you get older you will realize people would rather see you: fail than succeed, falter not finish, give up instead of getting up. But you are now wiser than last year- so brush off the haters and use the naysayers hate as your fuel.*

68 *Impossible is the unwillingness to try something.*

69 *The only competition we have is the limitations we put on ourselves. Once our mindset changes the momentum can't be tackled, the freight train won't be stopped and your heart will flow with love, sincerity and passion to not only accomplish goals but to help those who need a hand.*

*70 Once there were days I woke and saw
sunsets wishing today was over.
Wanting it to be tomorrow- praying
for strength, sad for my new normal,
crying for yesteryear, speck of light
in the distance, hope held me up,
darkness behind me, sunrise on the
horizon.*

71 Acceptance of the status quo is the acceptance of not trying.

72 We all have our burdens and challenges-no humans are perfect. Therefore don't judge others by their shortcomings but rather appreciate their successes and accomplishments.

73 Education is great but not when it becomes procrastination.

74 *It's never too early in the morning to start chores.*

75 *True wealth is not what car is parked in the driveway or the house we live in but rather our mental and physical health that we are blessed with every day.*

76 *When your wife is a nurse you are reminded daily of your blessings.*

77 Create solutions.

78 Surrounding yourself with like-minded people produces like-minded results. Surrounding yourself with smarter people with other knowledge and experiences from yourself creates true change.

79 The gift of life is life.

80 It's what we do with our time on Earth that will define if we truly lived.

81 God places opportunities and challenges in front of us to guide us toward our true destination in life.

82 Having the same job your entire life isn't a bad thing unless it's the wrong job.

83 *The unknown is an opportunity to dream and imagine so don't be scared.*

84 *Just because you're good at it doesn't mean you should do it.*

85 I know from personal experience I didn't succeed from sleeping and ignoring life but by living life.

86 People can smell sincerity

87 Love him for who he is and don't be upset for what he is not.

88 Douchebags are people who think they are doing you a favor for something they should have already done.

89 We can't make sense out of nonsense.

90 Thank you for being sunny when I can't see the sunshine.

91 I am in a cul-de-sac and there is nowhere to go.

92 Concentrate on your next step not your final step!

93 Instead of defining success by a finish line, a salary, a metric, a house, a car, or the followers and likes on a social media profile ---define success by the employment you enjoy that leaves you fulfilled, satisfied and happy.

94 An ode to my palm tree mug
Every Morning
Resistant to heat
Years of sipping
The day has come
Now stained and cracked
Like the palm weevil to the palm tree
Your best days were yesterday
Time to hold pens
You'll sit on my desk
Thanks for the memories
Thanks for the sips.

95 Time ticks
Watches turn
Clocks click
Minutes burn like embers at a
campfire
We all will burn out just don't know
when
Our legacy is shared
Our journey comes to an end
Our last step is taken
Yet – we live as though tomorrow is
guaranteed and our time here will
never stop.

96   The sun rises every day but it's always brighter when you're by my side.

97   There is light along the darkest trail.

98   An Arborist walks daily with some of God's greatest creations.

99   Your hugs are worth a thousand words and your words are priceless.

100   Lost on the trail is better than being lost in life.

101   When we fall in love with peoples' imperfections it creates a perfect relationship.

*102   We all have demons- it is how
we deal with our demons that make
us who we are.*

103   Listening takes patience.

*104   Luck is when preparation and
hard work are given an opportunity.*

*105   Sometimes the best thing said
is nothing.*

106   We live in an unnatural natural environment created by pesticides, fertilizers and urbanization. We created an ecosystem that was created from shortsightedness and selfishness. An environment that is not sustainable, short-lived, and will fail with long-term consequences affecting future generations. We have become kings of our universe and our ill-advised actions will slowly kill us.

107   With faith infinite possibilities
always exist.

108   True Joy comes from helping
others.

109   Happiness is not about how
much you have it is how much you
give.

110   Do the unknown and pull
yourself out of your comfort zone.

111   Have goals that wake you up
without an alarm clock.

112   Everyone starts at zero and some in the negative….its what you do that will define you.

113   Don't focus on the low tide because you'll never make it to the open sea.

114   When it comes to sales being second is ok because number 1 will eventually drop the ball.

115   GOD

Can't be grabbed nor touched
But He is here
Within the fabrics of our clothes
In the sixth sense of our
surroundings
In our heart, our brain
Within the wind, the rain, the surf
The top of our favorite peak
Beautiful, unimaginable yet visual
But cannot be described or
defined
We all need His faith
We all are better for it
We are better to each other with
Him
Don't be shy
Believe ---and—
Let Him in……………

116   *None of us are perfect but that doesn't mean we shouldn't chase perfection.*

117 Once we understand nothing is perfect we can then move on and make mistakes. The mistakes we make are not reasons to stop but rather our learning curve for a better way to reach our goals successfully.

118   A legendary warrior will always stay and never hide. Never run but just walk away. Never fall and be the last to die.

*119   Why does society insist on
taking and then not worrying about
what they have destroyed?*

*120   There is no main street without
a side street.*

*121   The challenge isn't being
independent, it's finding someone to
share independence with you.*

122   *I wasn't trying to be noticed but I won't be forgotten.*

123   *Learn from your mistakes and failures because they are correlated to your success.*

124   *Happiness is when you understand how lucky you truly are.*

125   *Simplicity is the foundation of success.*

126   *What is worse than deception-*
to be judged by a deceiver.

127   *The world is as big as you*
want it to be.

128   *Health and happiness can't be bought.*

129   *Age is chasing me down.*

130   *Being yourself should not be a struggle….being what everyone else wants you to be is a struggle.*

131   Life is Best When:
Highrises are trees
Highways are dirt paths
Roads aren't paved
Traffic is sticks and leaves
Smog is fog
Automobiles are legs
Rushing is relaxing
Music is birds calling.

132   Strive for perfection and if you
fall short you still achieve greatness.

133   *My definition of happiness is a state of acceptance for your unique situation. Through an outright release of all hate and equal inhaling of love. Not wasting time in controlling the uncontrollable.*

134   *Frustration is the result of miscommunication.*

135   *A landscape can be transformed one tree at a time.*

136   *The most important sense is common sense.*

137   Take what you can get and
        work with what you got.

138   Why do we live like we are
        guaranteed 75 years?

139 California sun smile down and take
        my hand. May your gentle ocean
      waves and warm beaches guide my
             uncertain steps.

140   Life is sometimes frightening
        but so is wasting time.

141   Life comes with no warranty.

142   Passionless work are called
                jobs.

143   Jealousy brings out the worst
                in everyone.

144   *The closest thing to wasting time is death.*

145   *Failure is like surfing...if you think you will fall off your board you will.*

146   Respect is earned through honesty, hard work and trust…yet the easiest to lose.

147 Dating and Surfing can be compared when it comes to failure….if you think that you will wipe out you will.

148   God has the answers-we just have to take the test.

149   We all travel different paths.

150 A domesticated cat is afraid to step
outside, not because it's not
curious but because its curiosity
may kill it.

151   When I close my eyes at the
beach I somehow see more.

152   A California sunset pushes today's problems out to sea.

153   Not knowing hurts more than not asking.

154   Time always wins.

155   To question life is normal …expecting an answer is not.

156   *You want to learn more than listen.*

157   A failure isn't the person who is trying it is the person who does not.

158   There is no such thing as certainty in life…yet we live as though there is.

159   Why can't you, why won't you…why don't you—No more excuses!

160   **Shadows always lumen over
the burning candle.**

161   **The truth sometimes lies
behind a closed curtain.**

162   **Confidence is faith in oneself.**

*163   A tree with water, soil and
sunshine won't grow if its roots are
girdled.*

*164   Chasing dreams is not crazy
NOT chasing them is.*

*165   The past is what I used to
do...the future is what I want to do.*

166   *Looking inward isn't hard; it's accepting what you see.*

167   *So much effort is lost to create a mirage.*

168   *Truth is painful but even worse is pretending it's all ok.*

169   *Live with no excuses and excuse yourself when the dumb execute.*

170 *As I age my eyes don't see as well and my ears don't hear that well but with you by my side everything is clear.*

171   *Thought of yesterday's failures then realized they are today's motivations.*

172   Complaining will always create chaos.

173   Contemplating takes time…even though quick answers are wanted wise decisions are never instantaneous.

174   Time exposes true intentions yet worse one's true colors.

175   A friend who is only there during the good times may not be a true friend.

176   When your daughter has a broken misplaced window screen in April you know it wasn't Santa.

177   Those who scream their views the loudest may be wrong.

178   Hate is hate -so stop justifying hate.

179   Trees are why I believe in God because a creation so perfect can't be explained.

180 *As a parent the most challenging obstacle is when you accept your child's differences of opinions and love them for who they are not what you want.*

181 *Those who see beauty in everything are the ones we need to fall in love with.*

182 *When you think you're done learning you're either lazy or delusional.*

183 *An apology is an honest step when you are wrong but insulting when done without true sincerity.*

184 *I hate arguing - it's a trail to nowhere.*

185 *Just say nothing - your loved ones will be appreciative.*

186 *My only goal my entire life for all my children: Plant, Water, Fertilize, Prune for Structure and enjoy watching them grow.*

187	*Watering a dead tree only moistens the soil.*

188	*Material defines what we own our actions define who we are.*

189	*Hoarding is a mental health issue. Be careful how you define your hobbies.*

190   Don't apologize for the locked
door.

191   Mentally on the mountain.
Physically in the valley ..we control
where our mind is.

192   Trust is hard to earn yet easy
to lose..

193   May your day be sunshine,
sunrises, sunsets and cool breezes.

194   *I used to be a grape but now I am a raisin.*

195   *I was grape juice now I am a fine wine.*

196   *Life's not about living in the past. It's learning from the past.*

197   *Roots were established yesterday; new leaves will start tomorrow.*

198   If you know someone who doesn't pick up their dog's poop while they are walking their dog…. appreciate their selfishness.

199   Dwelling on the past is the fuel to never move forward.

200   Inspiration fuels the imagination.

201   I will always look back and remember our challenges but I refuse to accept them as excuses to not move forward.

202   *It's not the vagina you came out of that defines who your mom is.*

203   *We are shaped by our past but don't let it define our future.*

204   *It's the people inside the house that make it a home.*

205   *Life's not about living in the past, it's learning from the past.*

206   Reminding a friend it's your birthday should remind you to find a new friend.

207   Prioritizing who you love should be your priority.

208   Spending time with a loved one is the best gift.

209 A true free society is when the people control the government not when the government controls the people.

*210   When you wake up next to
pure beauty it's tough to believe
what's outside in the world will be
better.*

*211   It's great to have people in
your life who believe in you but it
means nothing if you don't believe in
yourself.*

*212   Make time for yourself because
no one else will.*

213   *Give yourself grace and take a breather.*

214   *You accomplished so much today – look at what you completed, not what you did not- Count Your Wins!!!!!!!!!*

215   *Look at all the small things you conquered.*

*216   Friends don't show up with
empty hands.*

*217   Anger is a brick built on a weak
foundation, it's a matter of time until
it collapses.*

*218   The hardest part of being a
parent of an adult child is accepting
and appreciating each other's
differences.*

95

219   *My favorite lamp isn't the one
that creates the most light it is the
one that created the most memories.*

220   *When anger fills your soul walk
away from the fruit that created the
black flower.*

221   Watch out for the most popular person they sometimes are the most incompetent.

222   Be careful.....deception may get you what you want.

223   Friendships are fragile appreciate their seasonalities.

224   Life is delicate- appreciate all the minutes because each second is a gift.

225   *Accepting things we can't control brings peace to our chaotic lives.*

226   *Truth may hurt but always feels better than a blatant lie.*

227   *You are my light in a lampless room.*

228   Remember everyone will have ideas, suggestions and recommendations on what you should do in life but at the end of the day do what's best for you.

229   The road of life is never straight. You will run out of fuel, hit a pothole and get a flat tire but it's how you react to life's adversities that will define your destined direction.

230   *Today is just the beginning of endless possibilities- - enjoy the ride of life.*

231   *I sometimes surprise myself with what I wrote.*

232   *Believe in yourself because no one should care more about you than yourself.*

233   *Swim through turbulent seas because it won't last forever.*

*234   Most trees were here before us
and may outlive us, imagine what
they seen.*

*235   Remember Me Not for my
material but memories we made, Not
for what I acquired but for my
actions, Not for my uneasiness but
for my uniqueness, Not for my
imperfections but our perfect
moments, Not for what we didn't
finish but our finishes. Time will fade
away todays pain but it can never
take what we had in our hearts.*

236   *The toughest challenge of parenting is not giving advice.*

237   *The older I get, the more funerals I attend.*

238   *If you're sad walk your dog.*

239   *You're only good as your word and handshake was once a common saying ….. what happened?*

240   *Similar isn't exact and has turned into the new normal.*

241 *A true-life cycle is a forest.*

242 *Don't judge yourself by your failures but rather the lessons you learned.*

243 *Time Steals Opportunities.*

244   *I love where today can bring
me yet I miss yesteryear.*

245   *Time isn't your friend it's your foe.*

246   Walk into the woods and when you get to a tree that grabs your attention stop.

Close your eyes, take a deep breath and listen for a few minutes and open your eyes.

A forest is an example of how an ecosystem shows the different stages of life.

From a sapling to a mature tree we witness a never-ending performance of life, death and rebirth.

We see different stages of life playing out in front of us, under us, next to us and over us.

Some trees diseased from insects, fungi or bacteria are wrapped with beautifully colored mushrooms.

Other trees are rotten on the ground decaying and giving back to Mother Earth.

A wood of trees is in constant flux where movement of the lifecycle from birth to death isn't waiting for any observer.

It is the definition of life, survival and beauty.

*A tree appreciates its family all
rooted together and communicates in
various ways that are magical and
inconceivable to most.
From transpiring, releasing of odors
and rustling of their leaves are
examples of how trees speak to each
other.
It's not perfect because nothing is
but it's a perfectly executed living art
that is on display to enjoy, respect
and protect.
Providing clean air, food and shelter
for all living species, it's a perfect
place to walk to remind us that we
are not perfect.
When a tree root trips us on a hike
the forest humbles us and places our
problems back into a realistic order.
A forest shows us how we need to
appreciate our lives and how delicate
our lives are.*

*A forest shows us how we truly affect those
around us through our actions and more likely
our inactions.*